Grand Bruit
A Treasured Memory

Marilyn Billard

Order this book online at www.trafford.com
or email orders@trafford.com

Most Trafford titles are also available at major online book retailers.

© Copyright 2012 Marilyn Billard.

All rights reserved. No part of this publication may be reproduced, stored in a retrieval system, or transmitted, in any form or by any means, electronic, mechanical, photocopying, recording, or otherwise, without the written prior permission of the author.

Printed in the United States of America.

ISBN: 978-1-4669-4499-2 (sc)
ISBN: 978-1-4669-4501-2 (hc)
ISBN: 978-1-4669-4500-5 (e)

Library of Congress Control Number: 2012912903

Trafford rev. 07/16/2012

 www.trafford.com

North America & international
toll-free: 1 888 232 4444 (USA & Canada)
phone: 250 383 6864 ♦ fax: 812 355 4082

CONTENTS

Chapter 1: Trip to Grand Bruit, April 1972 1
Chapter 2: In Love 8
Chapter 3: The Proposal 14
Chapter 4: Our House 18
Chapter 5: Our Wedding 20
Chapter 6: Our Married Life Begins 23
Chapter 7: Getting to Know My Billard Family 25
Chapter 8: My Pregnancy 28
Chapter 9: Waiting for My Baby 32
Chapter 10: Bringing Jodie Home 36
Chapter 11: As Jodie Became a Child 38
Chapter 12: Taking things into My Own Hands 42
Chapter 13: School in Grand Bruit 46
Chapter 14: My Volunteer Works Begins 49
Chapter 15: Our Medical Clinic 53
Chapter 16: Our Church Project 70
Chapter 17: Local Service Does Good Work 72
Chapter 18: Meeting a New Friend 76
Chapter 19: Making Our Own Fun 79
Chapter 20: Sickness Comes to Grand Bruit 83
Chapter 21: My Job 86
Chapter 22: Summer Life 89
Chapter 23: Rumors 92

DEDICATION

To my sister in laws Loretta and Sheila Billard who was a big part of my life you both will always be a part of my heart your family misses you and i miss you both.

CHAPTER 1

Trip to Grand Bruit, April 1972

GRAND BRUIT WAS A PART of me before I was born. My mother came from that beautiful community with the jelly bean-colored houses, green green grass, and a most beautiful waterfall cascading down over the big boulders and running out into the sea.

My mother told me many stories of Grand Bruit when she was a child growing up there. Her brothers and sisters didn't have a lot. They had what they needed to survive—they had food, shelter, and two sets of clothes, one for weekdays and one for Sundays.

Food was, of course, grown and stored for the winter. I remember my mother telling me, if her dad, my grandfather, had a bad year fishing, they were issued food stamps to go get flour and molasses. As for meat, they hunted moose, birds, and caught fish to dry for the winter.

She would often tell me of her schooling, how they had to remember what was written on their slates, not exercise books. They had to remember it so they could move on to the next subjects, which were the basics: math, English, spelling, and maybe science.

My mother wanted me to know about Grand Bruit, and I never got to visit the community because my father was always working, and it cost way too much on the coastal boats to travel, plus having to take our family of six and go stay with another family for a week was all a bit too much. So I missed visits to Grand Bruit as a child.

But in April 1972, my friend, I'll call her Joan, asked if I would like to go with her to Grand Bruit for the Easter school break. I asked my mother, and she told me to sit down and write a letter to my Aunt Hannah and Uncle Isreal Billard and ask them if they would take me for a week; if they said yes, then I could go. I did exactly that and mailed the letter, waiting for the answer to return, which it did a week later.

I was so excited, packing my suitcase, getting everything ready for my big trip. Dad took me out to the CN boat, the *Tavernor*, and my friend Joan and I set sail for Grand Bruit. It was four hours on the boat, and boy, was I ever seasick. More than once, I wished I never stepped aboard the MV *Tavernor*.

After four long hours of throwing up, we made it to Grand Bruit. My uncle was standing on the wharf to meet me. I knew him because he came to our house in Burgeo for his doctor's visits twice a year. He was not a young man by then, but he stood straight with a smile on his face and strings of white, not gray, snow white hair hanging down his face.

I was so happy to put my feet on solid ground again. My uncle gave me a big hug and picked up my suitcase and off we went to walk to the other side of the harbor where they lived. My friend's brother-in-law was also there to meet her as her sister was home with the children.

As we entered my Aunt Hannah's house, I could smell something good cooking, also the strong smell of boiled tea, not tea bags, but boiled loose tea. I couldn't wait to get something in my stomach; boiled tea would do the trick, and it did indeed.

We had supper, and my aunt showed me to my room. She told Uncle Isreal to bring in my suitcase and put it in the bedroom. When I looked, here was this big iron bed with a huge feather mattress on it. Did it look inviting? Believe you me, I wanted to jump right in and cover myself up in my aunt's old handmade quilts that she had on the bed. No matter how upset my stomach was from being seasick, at sixteen years of age, I wanted to go outdoors and have a look at the community.

My aunt was not about to let me go without a little talk first. She told me, "Now, my dear, we don't stay up past ten o'clock, so you got to be in the house before that." I said, "OK, but I would rather ten thirty or 11:00 p.m." But I was staying with them, so I had to abide by their rules. She also made it clear that you don't go nowhere until the supper dishes are done.

We went into the pantry because there were no cupboards in the kitchen. Nobody had cupboards, only a pantry with shelves built on the wall and a little strip of wood nailed across to keep the plates from sliding down. We did the dishes in a plastic pan and hung the cups on a cup hook that was screwed into the wall. It was a very well-organized pantry.

I asked my aunt where my friend's sister lived, and she went to the window and pointed out the two-story house on the hill, next to a huge boulder. I got dressed, brushed my teeth in ice-cold water from the barrel, and left to go visit my friend's sister, who had two little children a couple of years apart, who were girls. And I remember to this day, the first time I saw them—beautiful curls in the oldest girl's hair, just like the curls of gold, and the baby was only two months old, but I can see her in my mind now, with a lilac dress and panties to match over her diaper. She was a very cute baby.

My friend and I played with the kids for a while, had our snaps taken with them with a Polaroid camera, and we were off outdoors to make new friends and to meet some of my cousins who I had never met. We decided that we would go for a walk and see where the other young people hung out. We could see, from the hill where my friend's sister lived, that there was an island with one house there and a graveyard. I later found out that it was called a breakwater, which kept the boats safe in the harbor from the raging sea of our shores.

We walked across the breakwater, and there they were, the younger men and women of Grand Bruit, hanging around and carrying on. We kind of stood there until someone asked me my name. I scanned my eyes over all the young men there, and my eyes met the eyes of a young man I knew was a bit older than me. He had long black hair that touched his shoulders, a jean jacket on a plaid suit, which was blue, and I will never forget that his jeans were snug with bell-bottomed legs.

I thought to myself, *I like the look of this fellow.* Myself at sixteen was slim with long black hair. I wondered, *Does he have a girlfriend, or would he be interested in me? No way.* He ignored me for a while, but looked at me when he thought I wasn't looking at him. It was a cold April night, and I had my mittens on. We were about to leave the breakwater when he came over to talk to me. He asked me how I was, and if I got sick on the boat. Then he got to carrying on with me and took my mitts and was pretending he was going to throw them in the water. I loved the attention. Who wouldn't? He was a handsome young man. He threw my mitts to me, and not being fast enough, I didn't catch them, and they did go over the breakwater. He felt bad about that, so he asked if he could walk me home and gave me his gloves to wear, and I said yes. I was in a world of my own. I didn't hear or see no one. I had a date with this young man with long black hair, who had bell bottom jeans on.

I wouldn't let him walk me all the way home to my aunt's house because she always peeks through her curtains, thinking no one can see, but you can. And I didn't want to be caught with a date on the first night because I knew that if my aunt caught me, she would write a letter to my mother before I got home, so we stopped on the Brook Bridge, overlooking the falls, and he kissed me good night. He watched me as I made my way down the road in the dark as there were no streetlights back then.

I couldn't sleep that night, I was so excited. I twisted and turned until the wee hours of the morning. When I finally did sleep, it was time to get up as no one sleeps past 7:30 a.m. in Grand Bruit. Everyone was out, buzzing around doing their work—men going out in the boat and women getting their children ready for school.

CHAPTER 2

In Love

My week in Grand Bruit went fairly fast, but it was a wonderful week. Bruce and I dated for the whole week, and we promised to write letters to one another as the only phone in Grand Bruit was a mobile phone that was installed in someone's house; but when you talked on the phone, everyone in the house could hear your conversation, and when you finished talking, you had to say, "Over."

It was a sad day, that day leaving Grand Bruit. Leaving a man I had just met, not knowing when we would see each other again; plus Bruce was getting ready to go back to his work, which was on the boats that sailed the Great Lakes, and he would be gone for eight or nine months. He said maybe he would get home for a month in the summer, then no more until December.

I thought to myself during the four hours on the MV *Tavernor, he will never write to me or keep in touch.* Needless to say, I had mixed emotions if this was going to flourish or just die. When I arrived in Burgeo, my father was there to pick me up, and as soon as I got into our house, Mom said to me, "So you have a boyfriend?" I looked at her so amazed. She said, "You may tell me because I know." I asked her, "Who told you that?" She said, "Aunt Hannah called on the mobile phone when the boat left Grand Bruit."

I said, "Very good, Aunt Hannah. I suppose, she told you who I went out with?" My mother said, "Yes, and I know who owns him, they are a good family."

I thought to myself, *So far so good, my mother doesn't seem too upset over it.* Then she went on to tell me, "Now if you get pregnant, I will not take the baby. I will look after it for you to work, but the minute you come through the door, the baby is yours." I said, "Mom, I didn't do anything. I won't be pregnant before I get married. I can assure you, if a man wants me, he will wait for me until our wedding night. I suppose you think I did something?" She said, "I'm just warning you, not telling you, and I hope you stick to your promise. There is enough of that going on around here now."

The next day, I asked Mom if I could get a copy of the post office key so I could go get my own mail, which was only going to be letters from

Bruce. It wasn't long before I got my first letter. I couldn't believe how good he could write. What a beautiful writer he was. He told me how happy he was to have met me and wished I could have stayed longer. He told me he was leaving the next week to go away to go to work. *Oh my!* I thought, *What will happen now?* My heart was broken. He went on to tell me he wanted me to come over when he came home this summer, and I could stay at his brother's house. I was so happy about that.

Bruce went back to work, and as soon as he did, he started writing letters to me. Every two days, I would get a letter from a different place, wherever his boat stopped. He would mail letters from places like Detroit, places in Ontario, and from all over. I would read them over and over, and I cherished each one of them. I counted the days for July to come to be able to go to Grand Bruit and see him. I wrote to his brother's wife to ask if I could come over when he came home. She wrote back and said, "Yes, you sure can, and by the way, I am your cousin." She went on to tell me that my grandfather and her mother were siblings. That suited me just fine. When I asked Mom about her, she said, "Yes, maid, she's our people." And Mom was happy that I was going to stay with her.

July came. I went to Grand Bruit to meet my handsome boyfriend, and there he was, standing on the wharf, waiting for me. We picked up my suitcase and started to walk to his brother's house. I was a bit nervous, not knowing them very well, but Bruce assured me they were very nice people, who had three children and another one on the way. We got to their house. Bruce introduced me to his brother and his wife. I felt so at home right from the start. That's how she made me feel.

We had supper, all of us. Bruce stayed as well, and Bruce and I played with the children. They had one boy and two beautiful little girls, all their names begin with B. I remember the youngest little girl climbing up in the rocking chair. She wanted to rock all by herself, but her mom was scared she would fall, so she went and got a belt belonging to her robe and tied the little girl in the rocking chair so she wouldn't fall. The little girl was delighted. She rocked and rocked as we washed the dishes.

When all was done, I thanked the family for supper and got ready to go out for a walk with my boyfriend.

We walked across the breakwater and stood there for a while, talking and sneaking a few kisses when we thought someone wasn't coming, as everyone used to walk across the breakwater for walks in the summer, plus the fact that Bruce was shy, and I myself would not kiss him if I knew someone would see us. That was not done in public back then. It was so good just to hold his hand. We had grown close through our letters we had written to one another.

We went to visit some of his people and his mom and dad. I liked them from the beginning and grew very close to the ones living in Grand Bruit. Bruce had sisters living in Port aux Basques area and Burgeo and Nova Scotia. He was from a family of fifteen, counting his mom and dad, having lost a brother that he never knew. His little brother died as a baby, but he was close to his six brothers and six sisters. Bruce was the fifth child.

His mom and dad worked hard to feed their family. His dad went away to work while his mom tended to everything at home, from doing all the gardening and drying the fish, to caring for her children and the house; but her boys, as they grew, helped them all they could. As they got work, they would buy things for their mom and dad, like table sets, a new stove, and whatever they needed.

Their daughters, some of them living in Grand Bruit, were always checking on their mom and dad and helping them in any way they could.

I continued to go to Grand Bruit, as well as Bruce continued to come visit me in Burgeo. Bruce's sister-in-law, whom I stayed with on my visits to Grand Bruit, became very close friends with me. She came to stay at our house when she was ready to have her fourth child. I was scared to sleep with her because I had caught the measles and she was pregnant. But her doctor told her she was far enough along and that it would not hurt the baby.

She wasn't there too long when she gave birth to yet another little baby girl who had blond hair, which was quite different from the other three children who had dark brown and black hair. She stayed with us until she felt well enough to travel with her baby back to Grand Bruit.

We had a letter from her a week after she went home to tell us she never got the measles, but the baby had them. I was scared, thinking the baby might get sick, but she never got sick.

CHAPTER 3

The Proposal

WE CONTINUED DATING FOR TWO years. By this time, I had foolishly quit school in grade 11. I had no interest in school; I never liked going there. So I went to work in the hospital as an untrained aid, knowing that if someone came there, a trained girl, I would lose my job; but I dearly loved working there, learning and seeing how the doctors and nurses worked with people. I always volunteered to go in the delivery room, a room where all babies were born into. I enjoyed doing what I was told to do.

This day, when I got off work at four, I went to the post office to see if I had a letter from the Great Lakes, and yes, of course, there was a letter there. I could never wait until I got home to read it. I would read it on my way up the road. The more I read this letter, the more excited I got. Bruce had asked me to get engaged, and if he had time on his way home next week, he would buy the ring. I couldn't write back because he would not get the letter before he left. I would have to wait until I saw him and give him my answer.

I never told Mom at first. I went out with my two best friends who lived in the Reach, and I let them read the letter. They were just as excited as I was. That's what I wanted—a man and a family. I got ready on my time off from the hospital and went to Grand Bruit to meet Bruce. He got home the night before I got there. When I saw him, my heart skipped a beat a few times because I knew that night I would get my ring.

We went for a walk up in the Arm, a dark place where the young people used to hang out. There was a big old boat that they called the Punt. As you walk up there, you are met with total darkness. I clutched Bruce's hand so tight because the young fellows often hid in the long grass and would make weird sounds just to scare the girls. As we got closer to the Punt, I said to Bruce, "There is nobody up here." He said, "Yea, I think there is. They are being quiet." As we got closer, someone flicked a cig butt out over the Punt. That's the only way you would know. We joined them for a while.

About eleven o'clock, we left to go home. I couldn't wait. We got to his brother's house and chatted with them for a while, then they said,

"We must go to bed and give you guys some time alone."

We sat and cuddled for a while. Bruce finally said, "I never got the ring." My heart fell. I asked why not. He said he had a direct flight and never had time. By the time he got to Port aux Basques, the boat was ready to leave.

Needless to say, I was so disappointed. He put his arms around me and said, "Don't worry. You and I will go to Port aux Basques tomorrow and pick out an engagement ring together."

I phoned Mom the next day. She was on cloud nine. Her daughter was getting engaged to a man from Grand Bruit, her own hometown. She was so proud, she loved Bruce.

The next day, we went to Port aux Basques and stayed at his Uncle Jack's house with his common-law wife. Our common friend was also staying there, going to school. We went to Alteen Jewelry Store to look at the engagement rings. I tried on a few, but my eyes fell on one I really liked. When I tried it on, it fit perfectly. Bruce asked if I wanted anything else. I said, "No." But he bought me two charms for my charm bracelet. One said, "A date to remember" so I could put the date wherein we got engaged, and he bought me our initials *M* and *B*. When we got back to his uncle's house, nobody was home, so he put the ring on my finger. That was July 9, 1974.

Bruce asked me when we should get married and where I would like to live, Grand Bruit or Burgeo? I said we would wait until I was twenty and that I wanted to live in Grand Bruit. He was very happy with both answers.

CHAPTER 4

Our House

A FEW WEEKS LATER, I received a letter from Bruce, but I was not expecting to read what he had on the letter. He told me he had bought a house next to the school for one hundred dollars. He went on to tell me that it needed some work and all new windows. He asked me to come over on my time off from work and see it. Everything was falling in place for me and Bruce.

I went to Grand Bruit the next week. Bruce's sisters and in-laws and his mom took me to the house. At first, I was not impressed, but like Bruce said, "It needs work." Then all of a sudden, his mom said, "I have some wallpaper leftover. I will go get that. If I don't have enough, my daughter might have a bit over there."

Bruce got some paint, nice white oil paint. He painted all the ceilings as they were all dark green, with pink doors. The house was very dark. Before I knew it, wallpaper was flying everywhere. So many women were papering each room, and the men were painting downstairs, tearing down canvases, putting up new stuff. The people who used to own the house had a small room in the porch where they kept bags and bags of coal, which they burned in the stove with wood and a bit of oil. The stove was called a k-Mac stove. Every day, you would have to throw out the ashes. This was going to be all new learning for me as I was used to an oil stove only.

Bruce said, "You will learn, don't worry. I will be home to show you." Within a few months, our house was ready to live in with new windows, a new porch, new paint on the outside, and a shed built for coal and wood.

CHAPTER 5

Our Wedding

THAT SUMMER, ON JULY 27, 1976, we got married, four years after meeting on a cold April evening. It was a beautiful day. Bruce wore a blue plaid suit, and of course, I wore a long white dress with a long train, and my dress had beads all around the waistband. We both had long black hair, touching our shoulders. We wanted to be married in August, but the minister was going to be gone for the month of July and August, so he arranged to have a student minister to come to Grand Bruit and marry us.

We didn't care, as long as we got married. For Bruce's mom and dad, having thirteen children all grown up, the chances of their family having a wedding held every year was good.

The year before, they had a son get married in 1975, and this year, another son was getting married, plus a daughter had gotten married a month before us on June 22, and on top of all that, my brother got married also a month before us on June 30. That year, everybody was wedding tired.

But whenever or whoever gets married, it was their day with their family and friends. I was so happy to have my mom, dad, brothers and sister, aunts and uncles from Burgeo come to my wedding and see our house.

I used to be the leader of the girl guide movement, the Rangers, for years, and on my wedding day, they all dressed in their uniform and sang "Ave Maria" for me as I walked up through the church. If they ever got found out that they had their uniforms on, they would have been in so much trouble wearing it for me, but I was so proud of them, and they did such an awesome job.

We all had such a good time at the wedding. Bruce and I thought we were going to have to put off our ceremony for an hour as our little flower girl, Bruce's niece, upon seeing us put on makeup, decided to put some on herself when we weren't looking. But she spilled it down the front of her dress. What a panic, but her mom hauled the dress off her, washed it in cold water, and put in the dryer. We were all in church, and here she came with our little flower girl, dress as good as new.

I guess things like that gave us good memories for years later. Bruce and I went to our new house to spend our wedding night. It was the first time

I had been with my man, or any man, and I was proud of it—nervous, but proud of it. People have not believed me, but the ones that knew me best knew I was telling the truth.

The next day, we went to the lodge where our wedding was to open our gifts, and Bruce's brother came to us and said, "You don't have to pay the band that played at your wedding." He paid them for us. It was the band from Isle aux Morts, Blue Waters, and they charged one hundred and fifty dollars.

There were one hundred and twenty people at our wedding. We had twelve hundred dollars given to us, plus gifts, such as things for our house, and to this day, I still have some of the dishes in my cupboard.

Later on the day, we received some bad news in our family. Our cousin's little boy, at age ten, had drowned in White Bear River. He was fishing, and the tide took him downstream. We knew the night of our wedding that there was an RCMP at our wedding, but we were told he was doing a routine check along the coast and came in Grand Bruit for the night. When we talked to him after we heard the news, he told us when he came ashore and someone told him there was a wedding, he decided to keep the news quiet until the next day. He did not want to ruin our wedding, which I know was very thoughtful.

CHAPTER 6

Our Married Life Begins

A FEW DAYS AFTER OUR beautiful wedding, all our relatives from both sides of our families got ready and went back home. It was sad for me because now I was staying back, and I had none of my family living there. Well, yes, cousins, and of course, my new family, the Billards. Most of all, I was going to miss my closest friend, not seeing her at all. That was difficult to adjust to. *Well*, I thought to myself, *we will talk often, and we will write letters to each other. We will never be far apart in our hearts*. But I had to be strong and go on with my new life.

A week after we got married, Bruce went fishing with a neighbor. He had no license for salmon or lobster fishing, so they took him on as a helper, and he would get a fair share of what was caught.

There were weeks when Bruce would bring home, in a little brown packet, a good week's pay, and there were weeks when the fishing was not so good. He would either not get paid or get very little pay.

That's how fishing was and still is today. Fishing is a gamble, but we learned to save when there was a good week for the week that came and there was little pay. I was taught by my father not to spend more than you make, and as he would preach that to all my brothers and sisters, I never, to this day, have forgotten it.

About a month after we were living in our house, Bruce's mom came down to our house one day with a suitcase full of everything. She handed it to me and said, "This is yours now." I asked her, "What is it?" She said, "I don't know, a suitcase that belongs to Bruce. I'm going to be bringing down here whatever he owns, now he got his own house." That's how his mom was. "Do what you want with it." I said, "OK, bring it down." And bring it down she did—clothes, radios, stereos, tapes, whatever she thought was Bruce's. She said, "When they get married and get their own houses, then they take their own things." And she was right. She had a small house with three bedrooms upstairs and one downstairs. Where did she store everything? No one knows, but Mother Clara, God love her.

CHAPTER 7

Getting to Know My Billard Family

I WAS ALWAYS A BIT scared to go into in-laws' houses without Bruce, but when I did, they welcomed me with open arms. As they got to know me, they would call in the mornings to come for coffee. I soon started to relax around them, and some of them had new babies, which was such a blessing—to go to their homes and get to take up in my arms the two new baby boys that were born that year. I became closer to some than others. I loved them all, but spent more time with the ones I was closer to.

In August of that year, I wasn't feeling well, and it scared me. Bruce had sent for a moose license for both of us, and we were both lucky enough to get one each. I didn't want to go because I wasn't well, but I went anyway. The next Monday, Bruce said, "You had better go to Port aux Basques to see what's wrong." I said, "Maybe I'm pregnant." I had not had my monthly cycle in August. Well, when someone goes on the boat, everyone needs to know "Why? What's wrong? Are you sick?" I thought, *I'm not telling them that I think I'm pregnant and make a fool of myself.* So I simply said, "I got to get some teeth out." They were happy with that.

I went to Port aux Basques, went to the doctor and had some test done. I had to wait until the next day to find out the results. I never slept that night. The next morning, I got up early and called the hospital. The nurse said, "Your test results were positive. You are pregnant." Wow! I never told no one. Then the phone was ringing at Uncle Jack's house. It was my mother telling me my brother's wife had just had a baby boy. I said, "Mom, I'm pregnant, but don't say nothing to nobody until I tell Bruce." She promised me she wouldn't.

I couldn't wait for the boat to leave Port aux Basques. I couldn't wait to get home that night and tell my husband he was going to be a dad. We would be in Grand Bruit around 8:00 p.m. When I got home, Bruce had supper cooked for me. When I smelled it, I got so sick; he had cooked moose liver. I asked him, "How come you cooked that? Where did you get the liver?"

"Oh," he said, "I killed my moose today up behind the church, and I wanted his liver for supper." He looked at me, "Don't you want some?" I was just about to tell him why I did not want it and why the smell was making me sick, when the door opened and his brother came in for a visit. I said to myself, *This will have to wait. I'm not saying anything until we are alone.*

I thought the world of my brother-in-law, but I couldn't wait for him to leave that night. He stayed and stayed; they had a few beers. I thought to myself, *If Bruce knew I was pregnant, he would drink more beer.* Anyways, around ten, my brother-in-law went home. Finally, I said to Bruce, "Do you know why I didn't eat that moose liver?" He said, "No, I thought you liked liver."

"Well, yes, I did until a month ago," I said, "Bruce, I'm pregnant." He said, "Are ya? For real?" I said, "Yes, boy, you are going to be a dad." He was very happy. We both were.

CHAPTER 8

My Pregnancy

IT WAS NOT A GOOD time for me being pregnant. Not the first few months. Was I ever sick. I remember Bruce wanting to go moose hunting, and he would not let me stay home alone because I was so sick.

He called my sister-in-law who had just had a baby boy and asked if I could come to her house to stay while he was gone with his brothers moose hunting. She was delighted, so off I went with my overnight bag. The next morning, I woke to the sound of a crying baby. My sister-in-law was bathing him, then feeding him. When she finished and the baby was all settled away, she got breakfast ready. The minute I smelled the toasted bread, up to the bathroom I ran—so sick I could eat very little.

The months went on. I got to feeling better, and by this time, winter had set in. Bruce was working on building a new breakwater. He always told me not to go outside if it was slippery, but whatever he told me not to do, of course, I did the opposite. I needed something at the shop, so I went over to get it. On my way down a low-grade hill to my house, I slipped and fell down on my back. I stayed there for a bit. By this time, I was six months pregnant. I just looked around to see if anyone had seen me. I saw no one, so I said to myself, *I'm not going to tell Bruce I fell down. He will get mad because he told me to stay inside.*

When Bruce came home for supper, he came in the door and said, "Did you hurt yourself?" I said, "Who saw me?" When he told me, I said, "I didn't think anybody saw me, and yes, I'm OK." I fell a few times that winter, but my baby was safe enough.

I went to my doctor once a month, whenever it was good enough for him to fly in. Our doctor would do his clinic at Bruce's aunt's house, which was right next door to our house. This time, when he came over, he told me I had to come down to Burgeo and get some blood done to see if everything was OK with me and our baby.

I went to Burgeo on the next boat. I had my blood taken, and the next day, my doctor called me back to tell me that my blood was RH negative, which meant nothing to me. She went on to explain that I would have to have this special needle seventy-two hours after I had the baby, and she went on to tell me that sometimes babies need transfusions. That scared me a bit. She went on to tell me that Bruce had to come down for blood work as well, to see what type he was.

Now, if you have ever seen a man panic, it was Bruce. He thought there was something wrong with the baby. I assured him it was routine, just in case I needed blood or the baby needed a transfusion when it was born. When the doctor flew to Grand Bruit the next week, Bruce came down with him on the helicopter. He was twenty-seven years old and having his first blood test. He was scared to death of the needle.

Once he got his blood work done, the doctor called us back to the clinic in Burgeo and told us that Bruce's blood was a complete opposite of mine. Very good, he is no help to me at all. The doctor told us not to worry if I or our baby needed blood, we would get it, but being new parents, we were worried.

The next day, we went home. It was the last of February, and was it ever cold, and frost covered everything. It was a late night trip on the *Tavernor*. My neighbor, who was also pregnant and due in June as I was, was on the *Tavernor* with me. When we got outside of Grand Bruit, the captain came to tell us, "We are putting down our anchor, and you have to go in the mail boat." I have never been so scared in my life. We had to walk down the gangplank, hovering over the water. It was a long gangplank, and two of the crew members were trying to keep the small boat close to the gangplank as it would move off with every wave of the sea. We had to jump on the boat, and they gave us blankets to wrap ourselves in. Then it was a fifteen-minute ride to Grand Bruit at minus twenty degrees at two in the morning. We arrived at the wharf. The tide was down low. Then we had to proceed to climb up more steps. Needless to say, when my head hit the pillow and I wrapped myself in my flannel nightdress, I was soon off to sleep with my husband's arms around me, keeping me toasty warm.

CHAPTER 9

Waiting for My Baby

As the spring approached and Bruce went back fishing, I was preparing for my baby. I wanted a little girl; Bruce wanted a little boy. I papered the spare bedroom. I never did it myself. My sisters-in-law did it with pretty yellow paper and yellow curtains to match. My sister-in-law told me I could borrow her crib and mattress. I ordered from Eaton's a few garments of clothes like PJs, little white slips, socks, and a sweater set. I needed a few things in the house for when I got home.

On the doctor's advice, I left Grand Bruit in April to go to Burgeo to wait for our baby on June 7. It was really due on May 18. Our little niece, who was my little flower girl, was so happy because her birthday was on May 18. It was a long wait from April until May 18. The doctor said I could go two weeks before or two weeks after. I just knew I couldn't wait.

Mom had a surprise baby shower for me. What a crowd. The house was full of my friends and Mom's friends. The baby things given to me were unreal. I thought my baby would never need another pair of clothes until it turned two. I had everything given to me from bottles, clothes, even a training pot, and the baby was not here yet.

April came and went. May came, and I was surely expecting my baby to be born on May 18, but that came and went. My doctor said, "You are OK, everything is good with your baby." My mother knew that I was anxious. She would say, "Marilyn, there is a saying, 'The apple will fall when it is ripe.' When your baby is ready, it will come."

"OK, you should know, Mom, you had four children."

On June 6, I went to bed at ten thirty. I wasn't feeling well all day. I had a lot of pressure. I couldn't sit for long, but I said nothing to my mother. About 11:00 p.m., I had to get up. My back was painful and everything hurt. When my feet hit the floor, Mom heard me and came out. She said, "Get dressed. You are going to the hospital." She called Dad up. He went out to start the car, but couldn't get it to go. He was in a panic. "We will have to call a taxi," he said, but after a few tries, he got the car going. He took me and Mom to the hospital at twelve that night. They admitted me. Hours came, hours went.

My pain was hard, but I was not moving forward. That was Monday night. Tuesday morning, the nurse came in and broke my water. Hours came, and once again, hours went. That night at nine, they took me to the case room, and after much pain and difficulty, at 9:45 p.m., our baby girl was born. Did I ever suffer, not because she was a big baby. She weighed seven pounds and six ounces. She had coal-black hair and dark eyes. She was beautiful.

I knew Bruce was waiting for me at his brother's house. I couldn't call him until 11:00 p.m. as it took the doctor an hour to stitch me up. He answered the phone with, "What did we get?" I was crying, "A little girl who looks just like you." He was so thrilled. Another happy person was Mom. She had it made. She had a nine-month-old baby grandson and a new baby granddaughter.

The next day, when I was feeding my baby girl, waiting for her dad to get there on boat, this little girl came to bed and got in bed with me. She was the niece of my friend whom I went to Grand Bruit with in 1972. She was about four at the time, and she knew me. Every day I spent in the hospital, she was with me. She loved the baby.

We had a task of coming up with a name. I had some picked out like Angie. Her dad wasn't fussy about that name.

Whatever we picked, my best friend's name was going onto it. We both liked Jodie, so we named her Jodie Marie Billard. Bruce was so happy, but would not pick her up. If I put her in his arms, he would hold her. He was scared she would break.

CHAPTER 10

Bringing Jodie Home

A WEEK AFTER JODIE WAS born, we got ready to leave Burgeo and go back to Grand Bruit to start our life with our baby girl. My neighbor had not yet had her baby. She was due the middle of June. I got home the next day. I was up putting clothes on the line at 7:00 a.m. My neighbor came down and made me go inside and rest. She put the baby clothes on the line. She was so good. A few days later, my neighbor had born a baby boy on June 16, and Jodie was born June 7. She already had a little girl.

Our baby was very cross. Later, I found out she had colic. Oh my, the days and nights I spent walking the floors trying to soothe my baby. I rocked across the floor many nights. I was so tired, and Bruce could not understand why I was so tired. He would eat his supper and go visit his friends and family. He would be gone some nights until 10:30 p.m. Bruce had a difficult time adjusting to married life, which meant staying home, helping with the baby, and giving up his freedom that he had for so many years.

One night, I was so tired, I said, "We need to talk." He knew I was upset, but after that night, he completely turned around and settled down into being a dad and husband. We went places together as a family after that. When Jodie got a little bigger that fall, I joined our church group, the United Church Women, in 1977. We did things to raise money for our church.

We only got to go to church once a month. The minister would come from Burgeo, and we never had church any other day but Sunday. We didn't care as long as we got a church. It was the custom that every year someone would volunteer to board the minister for free. Everyone was supposed to take their turn. Jodie was a month old before she was baptized with her little baby boy cousin.

CHAPTER 11

As Jodie Became a Child

As JODIE GREW INTO A beautiful little girl, I became more and more involved in my community. I got to know the people who lived there very well. I would visit them often and watch them hook mats and make quilts. What talent they had. They liked it that I joined the UCW, and I was willing to help when I could.

I got to know the teachers well, and I would ask them or tell them, "Call me if you need anything." We would get together at Christmastime and put on a concert together with my sister-in-laws and the kids from school.

When Jodie turned two, I wanted another baby. By the time I would have it, she would have been almost ready for school. She could have gone when she was four. She was so smart, and as Bruce and I started to take teachers in to stay with us, they spent a lot of time with Jodie.

In July of '79 I knew I was pregnant. I had agreed to take a teacher in to stay with us for that year. She was a beautiful young woman who had been there the year before but wanted to change her boardinghouse, so we agreed to take her.

She was a single woman, and she used to go out of town ever so often as there was nothing for her in Grand Bruit when it came to her social life. She met this young man one weekend and asked if he could come down sometime to our house. We agreed, but I was pregnant, and it became too much for me. Instead of a weekend, he was coming and staying for a week at a time. Bruce was fishing, and we had a spin dryer washer that we kept out in the porch. To get it in the house or kitchen, I had to lift it over a high doorstep to hook it up to the water taps. With Bruce's, Jodie's, my own, and the teacher's and an extra person in my house, I was washing every day, dragging this spin dryer in to try and keep the towels going. It was too hard and heavy for me.

It was the teacher's birthday in October, and I planned a big surprise party for her. It was too much for me to do, but I wanted to do it for her. Something special. My two feet were swollen, so during the party, I said to Bruce, they have to soon leave. It was 12:30 a.m., and I was so tired. Bruce said, "Go take a hot bath and get in bed. I will clean up and come up with you."

I went upstairs and ran a hot bath. It felt so good. I lay back, then all of a sudden, I got this vicious pain in my stomach. I got out of the bathtub, and I was bleeding. I called out to Bruce. He came running. He was scared to death. "What are we going to do!" he said. He called for the teacher to come up. She said, "Get into the bed, and I will call Corner Brook." Of course, they told her to get me out of there now. It was impossible since there were no boats until 10:30 a.m. the next day. Bruce, with the help of the teacher, did our bed all over with garbage bags and put nice warm flannel sheets on it. About an hour later, at 2:30 a.m., I felt a lot of pressure in my stomach, and it happened—I miscarried my baby. It was three months. The next day, I went to Burgeo, and my doctor confirmed it.

I couldn't dwell on it. It would have driven me crazy, so I just joined our local service district committee and became involved with that. I would help the teachers with the card games at the school and make sandwiches for lunch at the card game. The teacher asked me one night if it was her fault since I had so much work to do and that's what made me miscarry. I said, "No, I don't know what happened, and yes, it was too much work for me, but I don't blame you."

She told me those words, "I'm so sorry. I was wrapped up in my own world, I saw nothing, only my boyfriend." I agreed with her and said, "He can visit, but not too often." She agreed.

The local district committee decided to have a New Year's ball, but Mom wanted me to come to Burgeo for Christmas, so we went to Burgeo and went to the New Year's ball there. At twelve o'clock that night, when we were counting down, I asked Bruce what he expected to happen in 1980, this year. He said, "I have no idea. Why?" I said, "I know. I'm pregnant, and I am due July 9 or 12."

CHAPTER 12

Taking things into My Own Hands

Bruce was so happy with a second baby, maybe a boy this time. Everyone was happy when we told them on New Year's Day. Jodie was super excited.

When we got home and the teacher came back after her Christmas break, we told her. She was so happy for us. Then her boyfriend started coming back again. He kept coming back. We got tired of it until Bruce and I finally told him. "This is too hard on us." Bruce said, "This is too much work for Marilyn, and it's an extra mouth for us to feed." He got upset. He left our house at 10:00 p.m. on February and went to his home on boat, which was a three-hour run.

Bruce and I were so scared something would happen to him, and it would be our fault. We were worried. He called at 1:00 a.m. He said he was home, and he was sorry. We forgave him and never held it against him. They were young and in love. Nobody else existed in their world.

I was so proud of Bruce for doing that in a good way. He was taking care of his family. The teacher asked if we wanted her to move out because of this incident, and we told her no. She was a good person and a good friend to me.

Bruce watched over me. He would always go somewhere and then come back ever so often to see if I was OK. He would not let me lift Jodie if she fell asleep. He would take her up to bed.

I was not sick with this pregnancy at all, that's why I felt I was having a boy. It was so different. I kept a diary every month of how big my baby was and how he was growing, like getting fingers, toes, hair, and everything. I would lie on the couch, and Jodie would feel the baby moving all around. It was very active.

Jodie wanted a baby sister, and Mommy and Daddy wanted a baby boy. I went through the next nine months very easy, being very careful. In May, my doctor told me to come to Burgeo and stay until the baby came. They had told me I would have to go to Corner Brook to have the baby because of the difficult time I had with Jodie.

Jodie went with me, but she missed her dad a lot. He would come and get her for a few days. Take her home to Grand Bruit and then bring her back again. July 9 came, then the twelfth, but no baby. So on the fifteenth, the doctor sent me to Corner Brook to have my baby. Bruce went with me. His sister was also in there, waiting for her baby. We waited and waited. Finally, Bruce went home and brought Jodie to Grand Bruit with him. He was coming back in a few days.

On August 7, the doctor said we have to do something; this was too long. They made me drink castor oil, gave me a hot bath, and my labor started. Halfway through, it stopped. They had to give me the drip. It went on for hours until 8:00 p.m. On August 7, my beautiful baby boy was born, and two hours later, his cousin, another baby boy, was born. Both on the same day. My baby was eight pounds, nine ounces. Big boy.

We had his name all picked out. Bruce loved the name Justin. First, we said Robert Benjamin after our dads, but his cousin was going to be called Robert. We didn't need two Roberts in the family, so we went with Justin Bruce, and his dad was so proud. The next day, Bruce came in Corner Brook with Jodie to meet his son, and Jodie, her baby brother. She wasn't happy he was a boy. She wanted a sister.

That year in 1980, there were four babies born. Justin, being the first on August 7. His boy cousin also on August 7. Then in September, a little baby girl came into the Billard family. And in October, another baby girl came. Wow, lots of babies. Lots to grow up with and play with, and that they did. Our children had cousins all over Grand Bruit.

As they got older, they got to know each other. Sometimes, they played together good, and sometimes, like their dad told them, three is a crowd. Don't work with three kids. Justin was a strong little boy. At a very early age of four, he learned quickly, with his dad teaching him to make snares and set them to catch rabbits. He would, in the fall, go with his dad to set snares, and in the summer, they would make gear with lots of hooks on it. Then went to catch trout for bait and set their gear in the ponds to catch eels, which they caught a lot, just for fun, down in Eastern Brook.

Jodie, on the other hand, was content to stay in her room, if she had no one to play with, and play school with her dolls, or just play with her Barbies. You would think sometimes there was a crowd up in her room as she would be talking to her dolls. She was never bored. She loved pretending.

CHAPTER 13

School in Grand Bruit

JODIE LOVED SCHOOL. SHE LOVED her teacher, who was fresh out of college. A young lady from Conception Bay Area. I had taken teachers over the years, but that year I said, "No, I'm giving it up." But the school board called me and talked me into it.

Bruce and I got ready to go meet the new teacher, who was coming on the new boat, the *Marine Runner*. When the boat came on the side of the wharf, I saw one of the crew members pointing at me. She later told me that she asked him which one of the women on the wharf was Mrs. Billard. She said, "That's who I am living with." The crew member laughed and said, "They are all Mrs. Billards. That's all there is here." So she told him, "Marilyn Billard." And he pointed me out to her.

She was very happy to get off that boat but sad to leave her brother who was going to La Poile to teach. We brought her over to our house and showed her the bedroom that was hers. I took her to see the kids as they were sleeping. Gone to bed for the night. When she looked in the bathroom, she was surprised. She said to me, "You have running water?" I looked at her and answered, "Yes, why? You didn't think we did?"

She went to tell us that she had did some research on Grand Bruit, and we had lights, but no running water. She said she found it in the archives in college, so I told her it was time to update that paper.

The next day, she went to meet the other teacher, as we had two in a two-room school. He was a man from down her way as well. He was staying with Bruce's brother and their family.

Jodie was so taken up with her teacher, she cried when Saturdays came and there was no school. She loved school so much. Justin got used to having a teacher in the house. He couldn't talk good. Talk yes, but not plain. He would sit on the bottom step of our stairs and call out, "Teacher, teacher?" She would say, "Yes, Justin. What do you want?" He would come back with, "Can I come up with who?" He couldn't say *you*.

Fishing was not good that year, and there was no money to come in until November when Bruce would get his EI, then only until May, so we charged the teacher $150 a month, which included everything, and I washed all her clothes. Things weren't costly then, like food, so back then, it was enough. We grew our own vegetables, and we always had lots of meat, like moose and caribou.

It didn't take me long to get to know my daughter's first teacher and to like her a lot. I liked all the teachers I had and became close friends with them all. This teacher seemed younger, and she was a bit homesick, missing her boyfriend, missing her mom and dad and brothers and sisters. Her birthday was in November, so I thought, *Maybe I should have a surprise birthday party for her with the schoolkids.* I got everything ready. My kids said nothing. I sent out invitations to them all, made supper, and a baked apple pie with cream for dessert. I called her to come down as I wanted to tell her something. It was after school. In the meanwhile, I had all the kids line up behind the door. She came down, opened the door, and the kids jumped at her with a "surprise, Teacher." Needless to say, she was overwhelmed. She couldn't believe I would do something like that for her. She became one of my best friends.

CHAPTER 14

My Volunteer Works Begins

After joining the local district committee, we decided, in 1985, to have a Come Home Year. We knew (or did we?) what was involved in planning a big event such as this. There were no computers to help us, so we said, "We will have a meeting with the community, and if they are willing to help us, then we will set a year to have it."

We had our meeting with the community. They all agreed to help when we needed them and where we needed them. So we were off to a good start.

We set the date for August 1987 and two weeks, which we later learned was too long. We said, If we did it well, and it would profit much money, we would go to the government for help to build a medical clinic.

We also realized that the people on the local service were the same women on the UCW and local road board. I soon learned that once you volunteer, you are there for life, but I think you have to like it, or you don't stay with it. I loved it and still do years later.

Our local committee took control of running the community, like taking control of the streetlights as I used to go door to door, collecting the money every month. If we didn't pay for the streetlights ourselves, then we didn't have any, so the local district committee took it over and figured out what it would cost for each family to pay for it. It came out to $120 a year. The committee got a small portion of it.

You could pay it all at one time or however you wanted to, as long as it was paid before the year was up.

People were happy with that, and I did not have to go around asking for their money for the streetlights no more.

For two years, we made plans and tore up plans and made plans again for Come Home Year. After a while, it all came together. Everything was booked and invitations gone out. Government agreed to extra trips on the boat to bring people home. Our biggest worry was where everybody would sleep. We all had small houses. They couldn't stay at the school. That was needed for our suppers, our sales, and dances. We said, "Let it be. They will bring sleeping bags, whatever they need. It will be OK.

Some will bring tents. There are lots of lands to put tents on."

When the time came, boat after boat full of people came to our community. A lot of tears were shed, and there were hugs for everyone. People who had not been home for years came home. They were all so happy to see each other. Some of them had not seen each other since they were children. What a reunion on the wharf each time a boat came.

All my family came from Burgeo and Ramea. My parents, brothers and sister, and their families were staying with me, and my relatives from Ramea all brought their tents.

Our first night was meet and greet, and the next day, it started to rain and rain. I opened up my door, and here came all my relatives from Ramea. I had a two-story house with two bedrooms and a bathroom. They got rained out. What could I do? Bruce and I slept on the floor, and that night, when everyone was asleep, I went around and counted the people in our house. There were twenty-two people sleeping in the hallway, in the closet, kitchen, couch, porch. You had to step over them to get to the bathroom.

The next morning was crazy. I made one big bawl out. Everyone was quiet, and I told them, "I am on the committee. I have to be out of this house most of the time, so here are the rules: you feed yourself. If I don't have what you want, then go buy it yourself. Pick up your clothes, wash when you need to. I am not serving on you, and I need someone to watch my kids while I'm busy." They all agreed, and there were no problems.

We got through two weeks, and it was very sad to see them all go. After we got all our expenses paid for, the local service district came out with about $12,000 profit. Excellent.

CHAPTER 15

Our Medical Clinic

THEY HAD A PROGRAM IN Port aux Basques called Southwest Coast Development. It was run by a lady who became a good friend of mine and still is to this day. She knew her work. She called Grand Bruit and wanted someone to volunteer to go on a small committee in case we got funding from the government, and she would have someone in Grand Bruit to do the work that needed to be done. I believe there were a couple of people or more who also went with this program, but I was her contact person.

We had a meeting with our community and told them we were going after the government through Southwest Coast Development to build a medical center. Everyone was happy about that idea to build a place for our doctor, a proper clinic.

We applied, and it wasn't too long before Southwest Coast Development called me and said that the government was willing to pay for labor, but we had to pay for the materials. The local service along with the community agreed that it was a good deal. The government said it would be a top-up program for six people, and they didn't have to be all from Grand Bruit, so we hired three from Grand Bruit, two from Burgeo, one from La Poile—which was three young men and three women all in all.

Southwest Coast Development put my nephew as foreman, and I was put in charge of ordering materials. The lady came down with her colleagues and looked at the site we had picked out. They approved it, and now the work was to begin.

We did not know what type of ground we were dealing with. It was terrible. Shores from an old house, cement from an old house, and no bottom until thirteen feet down. We had to dig through sticks, roots, had to chop with an axe, and we had twelve of these holes to dig by hand with a shovel, and we only had a certain amount of time to do it.

Once the holes were dug with great difficulty, Southwest Coast came down with the men to inspect the holes before we poured the cement, and they turned it down. We had to dig down a little deeper; if we never hit bottom, we had to dig deeper. After much digging, we finally got to pour cement. Was that ever hard work. Once that was done, it was no time before the building went up. I had to order all the materials from Port aux Basques. Sometimes, we would not get half of it, so we had to go to our local shop and see what they had. All in all, we got it done. We had a good crowd of young people, and they worked hard. We had some laughs, but we were so proud of our project.

When it was finally completed, the Southwest Coast Development crowd came down and had an official opening with the cutting of the ribbon. Everyone in Grand Bruit was invited in to see the inside, and a lunch was provided. What a proud moment for the people of Grand Bruit to have their own medical clinic.

Within a few weeks, Burgeo Hospital fitted out the clinic with chairs, an examining table, things for the bathroom, a stretcher, a desk, and medicine cabinets. Wow! It was all ready for our doctor, and he was very pleased.

CHAPTER 16

Our Church Project

THE NEXT YEAR, AFTER THE clinic project, we went after one for our church as the roof on our church was getting bad, and we were lucky enough to get approved again.

Southwest Coast Development came down and looked at it and asked me if I would be in charge of ordering materials again. I said OK, and then the people were hired. Mostly young people, but they weren't lazy. We had a young fellow who was a real comic and made us laugh a lot.

Sometimes we slacked off a bit, but we did our work. Some of the older men in our community would come by every day to check and see what we were doing. Some of them figured it would never be done right because of the young ones who were working there. They didn't think they knew anything about putting a roof on. One man said when we got the roof on, "I won't spend much time in this church." We asked why and he said,

"The rafters are not right. They are too far apart. The roof will collapse after a time, with the weight of the boards."

That scared us, so I called for someone to come down from Southwest Coast Development and look at it. He did, and he said we were doing a good job, and the rafters were good.

We went on to finish the roof and to do the inside of the church. All the old pews were taken out, and new panel boards put on the walls. It looked so nice, except when one of our workers put the ladder through the new window. The ladder slid across the wall, and he jumped. Thank God he wasn't hurt. It was easy to replace a window, but not one of young men.

New carpet was laid, new tiles on the ceiling, new windows, and we asked the community to donate chairs and book racks instead of making new pews.

People from near and far donated chairs in memory of their loved ones. Some people donated three, four, and five. It was a great thing. Our UCW recorded, in a special book, how many were donated and by whom.

We had the grand opening of the church with our minister from Burgeo giving his blessing on the new building that we would use to worship God. A lot of people had their doubts about our work, but thirty years later, our church is still standing.

CHAPTER 17

Local Service Does Good Work

Our local service was always coming up with ideas to raise money. We had a good group working with us. We had card games at the school every second Saturday, as the school had them the other Saturday. It worked well.

The people of Grand Bruit would get their partners, go to the card game, and play ten games of 45s. Some people would take it very seriously and would go home upset if they didn't win. We always had something on tickets, and if the same person won two weeks in a row with drawing a name out of bag (you have no control of whoever wins), you would hear snickering from people.

It was a great fund-raiser. We would pick up prizes in one store one Saturday, and the other store the next Saturday. Then on Monday, we would go pay the bill and maybe we would profit $50; sometimes more, sometimes less.

I took over the local service committee in 1990. I tried to come up with new ideas to raise money. We had meetings, and among us all, we did have some excellent ideas. We worked well together. We had a winter carnival. It went excellent. We had all our games on the pond with Newfoundland music coming from the church windows where we had the stereo set up.

Bruce's sisters would come from far away whenever something was going on. They got to spend time with their mom, visit their brothers and sister, and enjoy whatever was happening. They supported Grand Bruit.

In the summertime, we had another big fund-raiser called Scoff and Scuff, which meant lots of food and a good dance. It was amazing. A crowd of Grand Bruit people came home, and like I said, they helped out where they could and supported.

It was a big job for our lady, who was our treasurer. She kept the books and did a good job. We always, at our annual meeting, got a letter telling and showing us what our money was doing, our take-in and our payout. It was a lot of work for her, but she didn't mind.

We got many summer student projects. It was supposed to be for students going to college, but they came down a level so we could put our students to work. I would, through Southwest

Coast Development, which did a lot of good work, get money every summer for about four years and hire four students to do minor repairs on the road and dig ditches. I had to be the overseer. Every morning, I would be up at 7:00 a.m., getting ready to go meet with the students and to tell them what they had to do.

I had to come up with enough work for them for six weeks. They worked hard, bringing clay in five-gallon buckets on a handbarrow from across the breakwater halfway around the harbor. It was heavy. Two students would dig the clay, and two carried it, then they would take turns.

If it was going to rain, I had to come up with an alternate plan of work, so I would send them to the church, and they would wash down the walls or do whatever. They were good students and did what was told of them to do.

One year, Trees Canada called me and said they were sending four hundred seedlings, trees of different kinds, and wanted to get some students to plant them around the harbor. Once again, this was through Southwest Coast Development.

First they said I could give each family four trees to plant by their door, and what was left would be planted around the community. Most people chose the pine trees, and the rest were planted near the waterfalls and from one end of the harbor to the next.

The trees grew big, and people took care of them. Some people liked them so much, one lady was visiting in Grand Bruit, and when she went away, there was one of our little trees sticking out of the cardboard box she had with her.

At the time, it upset us. We went to look to see where it was pulled from. Sure enough, we found it up in a place we called the Arm. After a while, we laughed about it and had a concert that Christmas with a skit about the missing tree.

CHAPTER 18

Meeting a New Friend

GRAND BRUIT WAS ALWAYS AN attraction for people who lived there to come home. Some came for a visit; some came all summer, as they had summer homes there. Grand Bruit was mostly known by word of mouth.

One of our residents had a shed he and his friends used to hang out in. They would have a cookout. Each man cooked their own, had a few beers, had a chat, and then called it a night. Many yachts came to Grand Bruit and went to the shed there. They got to meet people and write in the famous exercise book their names and where they came from.

Once, this couple built a bed and breakfast and opened up. They started putting their business in tourist books; it was a tourist chalet. Grand Bruit became known all over the world. Everyone who came to stay at their bed and breakfast loved Grand Bruit. They loved the people. Their accommodations were the best, and guests were treated with a home-cooked meal of fresh fish, or sometimes they wanted something different. They got fresh bread and good company.

There was a lady who, with her husband, purchased a house from a teacher who had left Grand Bruit. They came from the USA. They came for many years in the summertime, and they were everybody's friend. They loved hiking, boating, and hanging out with the people. After a few years, she told us she was selling her house to a friend of hers from New York and that her friend was disabled.

She asked me when her friend came, if I would help her with her luggage as she only had one good hand. I agreed to.

I went to the wharf to meet this lady, and there she was. My, oh my, what stuff she brought with her from the USA. I thought it was junk to me. That's what it looked like to me, but to her, they were antiques, and really they were. She loved old things.

We got it all carried to her house, and she said, "I will put it where I want to." I had cooked chicken for her for her supper. She loved it. Then she asked if there was anyone to do work for her in the harbor. I gave her some names, and I told her whatever I could do for her, I would. Her first task for me was to paper the house upstairs and downstairs, which was a big job. She brought the paper with her. It was the best wallpaper I had seen.

All the kids came to visit her. They were curious since they were not used to seeing somebody with a cane like she had. She liked the kids.

She got my son, who was ten, and another young man, who was dating a young girl, to come take up her carpet. She would make peanut butter sandwiches for their lunch. They loved it. She would give them a bit of money for helping her.

One thing I learned from the start, she was stubborn and had great willpower, but being like that kept her going. She could have, after having her stroke, gave up on her life, but it made her more willing to fight.

She supported Grand Bruit and the local service district committee. She came to all our UCW sales, and because she knew me, I would let her in school before anyone else was allowed in. I didn't let her in to be the first for the sale, but so she would not get knocked down, but she was sneaky and would look and pick out what she wanted to buy.

Over the years, I did what I could for her. I learned not to argue with her. I would lose anyway. She did things her way. She was a good friend, but a one of a kind lady.

CHAPTER 19

Making Our Own Fun

THE WINTERS WERE LONG AND dark. The men would be busy in the woods when they were home. Most of them worked in Hope Brook Gold Mine. The others fished.

Some of the women got together and played Rummoli while others like us got together. The six of us played a game of cards, 45s. We would go to each other's house on Wednesday nights, and play cards for prizes—first, second, and third prize. Whoever kept score always kept a diary. Whatever was going on in Grand Bruit was written down in our score book, from what the weather was like, to someone's death, to someone sick. It was all written there.

We would have a big lunch after—muffins, apricot pie, cookies, sandwiches—you name it, we ate it. We put on weight. How could we not? Plus, we drank wine that was "wonder wine" drink that we made ourselves. Some nights, we would drink slush. No one got drunk. Just a bit silly and loud.

One night, leaving my sister-in-law's house, we were laughing so hard. The boys in the shed having a beer came out, and one of them said, "Oh yes, they have been drinking that old 'wonder wine' tonight." We were happy that's all I know.

Another night, we had marshberry pie with cool whip, and when we were doing the dishes, my sister-in-law sprayed what I thought was cool whip because it was in a can. She sprayed it up my arm. It was white, so what I did was that I licked it all off and swallowed it. When I did, I tasted something awful. It was shaving cream. She played a trick on me. But when they all realized I ate it, they were so scared I would be poisoned and die.

I washed my mouth out, and all the way home, I was spitting. Before I got home, I had an idea to scare them back. We had a lot of snow piled up on the road, so I stayed behind, and when they weren't looking, I got down very quietly behind a bank of snow. When they looked back and I was gone, they started singing out to me. I wouldn't answer. I stayed still. They came back to look for me. When they found me, I was not moving. They thought I had fell over because of the shaving cream I ate. But I jumped up and scared the three of them half to death. What a laugh.

We did this every Wednesday. We noticed my sister-in-law was getting bigger than usual, then she told us she was pregnant and wanted us to go with her to our mother-in-law to tell her she was having her fifth child. So this Saturday, we all met at my house and went to my mother-in-law's. We started talking, and finally, one of us said that she was pregnant. My mother-in-law looked at us and said, "I don't care. If she is, she is."

We just blew out laughing. We were all thinking she would say something different.

Darts were set up in Grand Bruit, and whoever could go, went. Everybody enjoyed it, but like cards, there were very serious ones and some like me, who didn't care if I won or lost. Life was never boring in Grand Bruit. We had a harbor full of people and a two-room school full of kids.

It was so funny, my sister-in-law who was pregnant had her baby on Wednesday night—our card game night. Her man came over and gave us a bottle of wine, and we drank it. What a happy night.

Another card game memory is, one night, on our way home, we went into my shed to see our rabbits, as we raised rabbits for something to do, and Bruce had them in separate pens. But of course, I being evil that night thought, *I'm going to put them together for a while and see what happens.*

So I caught the male rabbit and threw him in with the female. Now, you want to see the fur flying. I got scared. I couldn't catch the male rabbit; he was having too much fun. Between the four of us, we managed to get a hold of him and threw him back in his own pen. I made the women promise not to tell Bruce. He would kill me.

Three months went by. Bruce came in one morning. He said, "That's strange." I had forgotten about what I had done. I said, "What's strange?" He said, "The rabbit got five babies in her pen." It came to me. I could not look at Bruce. I thought to myself, *I am going to have to tell him.* When I did, he never got too mad, but the sad thing was the five little bunnies died. I felt bad about that.

CHAPTER 20

Sickness Comes to Grand Bruit

As our people got older, they began to die. It was very sad. I had good people living beside our house. When my window was open, I could hear my neighbor singing hymns. He was a wonderful gentleman who had a wife who loved to write letters.

The seniors who lived on our side of Grand Bruit would watch for the little kids to come over to school, making sure they did not stop on the Brook Bridge. It was a bigger worry in the wintertime that they might slip and go over the falls. If the weather turned bad, the kids from the other side would come to my house or go to their nans for lunch. School was never cancelled.

One senior lady told me, if you eat grapes, you won't get cancer. But she did get it, and she lived for a long time with it the best way she could.

Seems like when our older people started to die, it would go for a couple of years, and then we would lose a couple more. It was very sad. Some lost their memories, some just went to sleep, but they were elderly.

When someone died, all the men would dig the grave. Everyone worked together well. It was difficult in the wintertime with the ground frozen so hard.

The women would make meals for the family and also go spend time with them and try to comfort them. There were no cars to take our loved ones in when they died, so in winter, they put them on a slide and pulled them over to the graveyard.

We understood what would happen as they got older, but we worried about what would happen to our community. They were the pillars of Grand Bruit.

Bruce's dad became very sick for two years, battling cancer, going to Burgeo, taking blood every two weeks. It was hard on his wife and children who lived in Grand Bruit and harder on his children who were living away. His children who lived in Port aux Basques area and Burgeo came to see their dad as much as possible. No matter how sick he was or how much pain he was in, when you asked him if he had pain, he would say, "Naw, not bad." But we knew the difference.

We had a minister who was very good to our family when my father was sick. He would pick them up more than once from the CN boats and take them to their daughter's house in Burgeo.

As the months went on, he got sicker and sicker. My sister-in-law and I travelled to Burgeo one Saturday with our children to visit him in the hospital, but when we got there, he was not doing too well. We came back again on Sunday, knowing he didn't have long to live.

On Monday, my sisters-in-law and I went to their mom's house to freshen it up, as we knew the family would soon be coming home for their dad's funeral. All of a sudden, at about 11:00 a.m. Sept 8, the phone was ringing. I answered it, and it was my sister-in-law telling me that her dad had just passed away.

My sisters-in-law lost it. They were so upset, and they cried and cried. Their aunt came in and told them to stop crying because their dad had been a sick man for a while now. In a way, she was right, but it is good to cry. It helps make you feel better.

I called the school to tell the teacher the news and to let his grandchildren out of school to be with their moms and dad. She called the school board and told her boss she was closing school for a few days. He asked her why. She told him, "I have to. This man died today, and all the children are his grandchildren except for two who are his niece and nephew."

CHAPTER 21

My Job

THE TEACHER WE HAD WAS the one who had lived with us. She had gotten married and was pregnant. She had asked me to babysit her baby when the time came to do so. I was very happy about that. I was a smoker, and when she told me she was pregnant, I quit smoking. I would not smoke around her. I gave up drinking coffee for nine months because she did, and we drank milk.

When the time came for the baby to be born, I got excited. Then when the baby came into the world, she was not well. She was born in Carbonear on September 24 and had to be rushed to St. John's. That was very difficult on Mommy and Daddy. Her mom had to stay in the hospital while the dad travelled to St. John's every day to see the baby, and he would take pictures of her and bring them back to Mommy. That's the only thing that kept her going.

After the baby got well, I was invited to come for her christening. It was a nice event, and she was such a strong baby. As the days went by, she got stronger. When they came home, her mom had to go back to teaching, and she asked me to babysit the baby. I was very nervous at first, taking care of this tiny little girl with her red hair and a mind of her own.

She was a quiet baby, and every Saturday, her mom would dress her warm, wrap her in lots of blankets, put her in her sleigh, and off we would go for a walk. We never missed many Saturdays. Her dad would go in the woods to cut wood with his students, and the women, with their children, would spend Saturdays at my house.

We would sit around the table, keeping warm around the oil stove, drinking coffee, and eating cheese and crackers. My sister-in-laws would pick up their groceries—lots of it—drop them off at my house and come in from one to five every Saturday. We became very close to each other.

We had our own little group, the same one we played cards with on Wednesday nights. We were always together.

I worked and took care of this little girl for a few years. I took her outdoors every day; it was fit to get out. She loved it. I took her visiting older people whom she loved to be around. Everyone in Grand

Bruit loved this little girl. They would go home for Easter and Christmas, and I missed her a lot when they did.

I tried to be helpful to her mom. I knew she was tired when she came home from teaching, so I would do most of her work so when she came home, she could relax and enjoy her time with her baby.

My husband and I became aunt and uncle to this little girl, and when they decided to move out a couple years later, it broke my heart, but I knew they had to do what was best for them.

My friend assured me that the baby would never forget me. She told me these words, "The baby will never forget the love you have shown and given her." And she is still a part of my life twenty years later.

It took me a long time to get over losing my friend from Grand Bruit and seeing her every day, but she was not lost in my heart.

CHAPTER 22

Summer Life

L IFE WENT ON IN GRAND Bruit. In summer, people came and went. Boats came to Grand Bruit and stayed for a few days. Kids came with grandparents who had summer homes there and stayed all summer. They had a little group formed and would spend the summer, having fires up on the Arm and swimming in the pond for hours and hours.

It was no trouble to see wet towels hung on clotheslines, waiting to dry, and go back swimming again. They would get together, the boys and the girls would hang out together, but at night, they all joined in for the bonfire.

They became great friends. It was always so nice to hear the laughter of the teenagers. Grand Bruit came alive in the summertime for a few months.

When the last of August came, silence filled the air. The kids were very sad they had to go back home. They would miss one another, and even though they would talk to each other over the winter, they would not see each other until the following summer. It was sad to see them go. We wished we could keep them all.

The men were busy cluing up the lobster season and preparing for the cod fishing. The women would be busy having meetings. Some of the more talented women were hooking mats and making quilts. No trouble when you walked down the road to hear a sewing machine humming. No one was bored. Moose hunting season was a big thing. The men and some women hunted to get their meat for the winter, taking care of their families.

The gardens that were set in the spring were dug up for yummy carrots, potatoes, and many other vegetables, and these were taken to the root cellars that they had built to store their vegetables for the winter.

Women, including myself, did beets, bottled jam, moose, rabbits, caribou, for the winter. We were always very busy in the fall. We would, for weeks, pick partridgeberries by the gallons and then go over across the breakwater and pick marshberries. We always had plenty of jam for making pies and cookies.

As the younger women got together, new ideas came to light. We would plan winter carnivals, which were enjoyed by all. Our children, who were away attending school in Burgeo and Port aux Basques, came home to attend this event and spend time with us.

It was so difficult for our children to be away from us parents and equally as hard on them, plus a big responsibility for the people they stayed with, but we did what we had to so they would get their education.

In the fall, Bruce and I, his sister and her husband spent a lot of time with each other. Every Sunday night, we would go visit our family. We never missed many Sundays unless it was stormy. Our other sister-in-law and her husband would meet us at her house. We had our own places to sit, and we earned our own mugs—Christmas mugs; nobody else used them.

Bruce's sister would offer us cake, cheese, and crackers. What a lunch. Her husband, God love him, would serve drinks to the men. We would be chatting and laughing in the kitchen while the men sat in silence, watching TV. They were most of the time silent. It was awesome to do this every Sunday night. We stayed for a couple of hours and then go to the house of Bruce's other brother to have coffee, which, most of the time, we never had because we were filled to the top. We chatted and stayed for an hour then moved on to another brother's, the one who was with us. It was a tradition that went on for years, Sunday after Sunday, even when we had church, we did this after that.

CHAPTER 23

Rumors

As time went on, we would hear rumors that we were going to lose our boats, the *Tavernor* and *Runner*. These rumors went on for a long time until it became a reality. We had many boats over the years that gave us excellent service. The *Marine Runner* was the fastest and one of the best.

Over the years, the boats brought many, many visitors to Grand Bruit in the summertime. Hundreds, over the years, came for Come Home Years, different events, and most often, to visit their families. A lot of people who grew up in Grand Bruit left to go out in the world to work and settle down elsewhere, still maintaining their mom's and dad's old houses, and some purchased old houses, which they repaired, repainted, and turned into beautiful summer homes.

We loved our boats. We got to know the crew very well, and they did favors for the people of Grand Bruit many times. I remember, on many occasions, when a loved one would pass away in Burgeo hospital or Port aux Basques hospital, the boats would wait if the family wasn't there on time for the boat to leave. The crew would do whatever they could on all boats to make it easier for the family.

When someone got sick in Grand Bruit, the boats tried their best to get there as fast as they could to get them out, and our sick people were treated with respect by the crew, offering a cup of tea or anything they needed or wanted.

I remember getting a big boat, the *Northern Ranger*. What a boat, just beautiful inside and out. But on the first visit to Grand Bruit, all the men said, "That boat is top-heavy. She's too light on the water, like a cork," they said. We found out later that they knew what they were talking about.

We had set up a small transportation committee in Grand Bruit. I and a few other people were on the committee. It was set up because the government wanted contact people in every community.

I was travelling one day on the *Northern Ranger*, coming from Port aux Basques to Grand Bruit, and there was a lot of wind southwest. Boy oh boy, did that boat rock from side to side and back up again. I was so sick, as well as everyone else on board. We got to La Poile, off-loaded people and freight, and headed to Grand Bruit, one hour away. I thought to myself, *I will be so happy when I step on Grand Bruit tonight.*

Before we got to Grand Bruit, a big wave hit the side of the *Northern Ranger*, and she went down, her side windows hitting the water. We went flying across the boat, life jackets were flying through the air. The mate came running for us to put on our life jackets. Anything that was loose had been tossed all over the boat.

After a few minutes, which seemed like an hour to us, the boat came back upright. As we pulled ourselves together from the big scare we just had, the captain came down to see if we were OK and asked if anyone was hurt.

Scared yes, but we held on tight. No one was hurt. I asked him, "Did the boat list out?" He said, "Yes. I didn't think I would get her back, but I did." He also had no color in his face.

When we got in Grand Bruit, I settled down. The next day, I called the minister of transportation's office to see if the incident was reported, but the man I talked to said it never happened. Now that made me mad. He said I was lying. He agreed it was a windy day, but this boat was very modern, and she could not be listed out.

That did not sit well with me, so I called a meeting with all our members, and we wrote a letter to government, asking for a public meeting in Grand

Bruit, and we wanted the captain of the *Northern Ranger* to attend this meeting.

About two weeks later, we received a letter from the government, telling us they would be there the following week. We called everyone in the harbor and told them when to meet at the school and what the meeting was about.

When they arrived, the captain from the *Northern Ranger* was there also. The meeting started, and the man from the government had an attitude right from the start. He denied that anything happened. Then it was our say, our chance to ask questions, seeing that I was aboard the boat when it happened. I directed my questions at the captain. I asked him, "You were the captain the day we came on the *Northern Ranger* and she hit a wave that sent her to the side with her windows hitting the water." He said, "Yes, ma'am." I said, "You came to us after, asking if anyone was hurt." He said, "Yes, ma'am." Then I asked him, "Did everything aboard that boat go flying out?" He said, "Yes." Then I went on to asking him, "Sir, in your opinion—and be truthful, did you tell us, you thought you were going to lose the boat because she listed out?" He said, "Yes, I did." I said, "Thank you for being honest." I was on that boat along with other people, and we knew—why would we tell lies? It was our life.

The government man went on to ask me, "How come you people know where that boat is at every hour of every day?" As I was head of the committee, I told him, "Because, sir, it is our business to know." I said "You can, in St. John's, go post mail when you want, pick up your mail when you want, you can go get your drugs, pick up groceries. All you have to do is drive and get it." He said, "Yes, but what are you getting at?"

I went on to tell him that we get our mail ready and post according to where the boat is, the boat brings our mail, it brings our food, it brings our drugs and when we find out that she is going to be here at a certain time, we have to be ready to go if we have appointments with the doctor. He never, until then, realized how an outport community worked. All he had to do was to get into his car and drive wherever, whenever, but he told me after that it was an awakening for him to see how people from an outport community live and survive without a car.

After that meeting was over, the MV *Northern Ranger* was taken off and put on dry dock for an assessment, and as the men said in the beginning, the boat was too light, and they poured cement in the bow of the boat.

Our vessel we had, the MV *Tavernor*, was a slow boat, but you could rely on her. You could get three meals a day, buy a berth if you had a long travel or if you had children or if you wanted peace and quiet, the cost was not high. If I remember, it was about ten dollars. The meals were so good, and on a nice day, I truly enjoyed them.

In 1995 and 1996, we received letters from our government, telling us we would lose the *Tavernor* and get faster boats, and instead of once a week, they would come every day. So a list of meetings would take place over the next two years for Grand Bruit and La Poile; both communities were affected by the boats.

Our local service committee together with our local transportation committee (as most of us were on both committees) started a series of meetings.

We received a phone call from Mr. John Efford, who was at that time transportation minister, that he was coming to Grand Bruit with his people to talk about the new ferry system. The people were excited about having a ferry every day, not knowing deep down that, that was the beginning of the end of Grand Bruit.

Mr. Efford flew in by helicopter for a public meeting with a proposal for us to look at and discuss, telling us that the two communities—Grand Bruit and La Poile—had to agree on a schedule, or this would not work.

We told him we wanted the main place in our schedule to be Burgeo for our doctor's needs, banking, church, and our kids who were attending school there. We wrote it up, faxed it to the transportation committee in La Poile. They turned it down flat as those people wanted Port aux Basques as their main place. They used Port aux Basques as much as we used Burgeo.

Right then and there we knew it was going to be a battle of words. We wanted what we wanted, and La Poile wanted what they wanted, which made sense. All the government did was upset both communities, which each one had a lot of friends there.

Over the next year, we went from one community to the next for meetings and more meetings, trying to come up with a schedule that would suit both communities. Grand Bruit, being the smaller community, had a lot to say when it came to the government. "Majority rules," we were told.

We were invited to Port aux Basques with La Poile to meet with Mr. Efford at the hotel. During the meeting, a knock came on the door. It was CBC and the Gulf news wanting to sit in on the meeting. Mr. Efford became very upset because they were there. He accused us of inviting them, which we did not. They have their way of finding things out.

It was a fairly good meeting, and a schedule was worked out. It was taken back to the communities to see if they agreed with it; then the schedule was the ferry would go to Rose Blanche on Mondays, Wednesdays, Fridays, Saturdays, and then return. Go to Burgeo on Tuesdays, and have a layover day on Thursdays. We would have liked more trips to Burgeo, but being the smaller community, we were outvoted.

We had to fight for a change if the weather was nasty on Tuesday and we didn't get to Burgeo, we would lose our trip. But that was changed to go on Thursday if Tuesday was not suitable. It worked out good.

People could now go out more often and see relatives, make appointments for haircuts, to see doctors, and do banking. Our people seemed to like it, not realizing what damage we would be doing to our little community. The more everybody went out, the more they brought back home. The more they brought back home, the less they purchased from the stores in Grand Bruit, and both grocery stores begun to suffer.

What was happening? They would buy items like toothpaste, butter, anything that was on sale, toilet tissue, paper towels, and they (myself included) wouldn't have to buy anything in Grand Bruit all winter. The freight charges for Grand Bruit stores were costly for the owners, and they had to have their markup prices a little higher. They couldn't afford to sell things cheap because they would have to buy items in bulk to do so.

No way could our two stores compete with the bigger stores in Port aux Basques and Burgeo.

The sad thing was when someone wanted something ordered from our stores and the store owners couldn't get it, they would get upset, but they weren't supporting their own.

Eventually, one store closed. Now that's not all that happened to Grand Bruit. Some of our younger people got sick. And for years, we had no one die, then maybe one or two elderly; then all of a sudden, people were getting cancer, and it took down a lot of our people. Grand Bruit was shaken every time someone died, old or young, as we were a close-knit community. We might have gotten on one another's nerves every now and then, but we got over it.

When our ferry was called for an emergency, in an hour, the boat was there no matter what time of the night it was. Nobody died waiting. We lost one gentleman who passed away aboard the ferry. He was elderly. What a nice man he was. The crew, the same as years ago, treated us all alike and helped when and where they could, and I have to say what a good crew they were.

As people brought more groceries home, the harder it got for the one store. It first started off with cardboard boxes, but later, everyone started using plastic containers. People also started taking their mail outside of Grand Bruit to be posted or gave it to someone else to do it for them. All of this led to the closing of our store and post office as well. Our postmistress retired after thirty-five years of service.

In 1997, our community hosted yet another Come Home Year, and it was a sad year for us as Bruce lost his job. The mine closed down, and against our will, we had to leave Grand Bruit. We thought about it long and hard before we did go. What were we to do? Go on welfare? I don't think so. We were both able-bodied people and wanted to work. I never cried so much before in my life, leaving Grand Bruit.

Bruce left in March to work at Nugget Pond on the Baie Verte Peninsula. I went down for a visit and thought, *Oh my, will I ever get used to this big community?*

I stayed in Grand Bruit until August. I was in charge of the local service committee, and I had a lot of things to clean up before I left, plus I was on the Come Home Year Committee.

What a wonderful Come Home Year we had in 1997, but for us, it ended so sadly with having to leave.

After moving to La Scie, many a night I cried myself to sleep, missing my home at Grand Bruit, missing my married family and my family in Burgeo. Every chance we got, we went home. I never looked for work because I wouldn't be able to go home when I wanted to.

Bruce would go to work on nights, Justin would go outdoors with the friends he had made, and I was home alone; whereas when I was in Grand Bruit, I was never alone. More than one night I said to myself, *I want to go home. I can't do this.* I packed my suitcase more than Bruce ever knew. I didn't think I could do it, to live down in La Scie.

Bruce looked forward to going home whenever we could. He always went home to fish salmon in Cinq Cerf River where we had our cabin. I missed going to our cabin.

Bruce and I went home in the fall to go moose hunting and rabbit catching, everything he did while we lived there. We always said we still live there but are gone away working. Bruce always wanted me to go to the cabin when we went home, but I didn't want to leave Grand Bruit, not for a minute. If we were there for a week, I wanted my week there in Grand Bruit, not at the cabin.

We always supported Grand Bruit even if we weren't there. We still paid our church, paid our fees for our streetlights, and continued having our mail go there for quite a while with help from our sister-in-law who packed it up once a week and sent it down to us. We gave her the money for postage.

Leaving Grand Bruit was devastating for us. I was close to all my sisters-in-law there and friends with them all, but there was one whom I always hung around with. Our families did things together. We went to our cabins together. We played cards on Saturday nights. Our children became very close to one another. She used to talk to me and I talk to her. We were good together. One time, she told me she wasn't feeling good and having trouble with her bowels. She went to the doctor. He told her she was going through menopause, which was because of her age.

This problem continued until she got another opinion, and they did the light and soon found out she had a tumor in her bowel. She called me that night and wanted me to come with her. Without thinking about it, I was packing my bag and heading for Port aux Basques. I knew it was going to be costly, and we never had much money. Bruce was getting laid off, and I had saved up $1,200 for when that happened, but Bruce said, "Take it all, Marilyn, and go."

When I got to Port aux Basques, my sister-in-law had the news. She had to be in Corner Brook the next day. Her husband was devastated as were her children. We went in, had her test done, and we were called into the doctor's office. He told her the tumor had gone through the wall of her bowel. Did she cry? No, she simply said, "Well, my son, it might as well just be me than anyone else. I guess it's my turn." What a statement. We asked different questions, and he said surgery was needed. She had her surgery, losing thirteen inches of her bowel, then went on months later with treatment with chemo and radiation. She was a trooper. I stayed in Corner Brook for ten days with her. She never wanted me to leave.

It was difficult being down to La Scie and her in Halifax. When she came home to Grand Bruit, I came home also to be with her.

A year or so after her treatment, she went back for one of her CAT scans and she wanted me to go with her to get her report. There it was, more bad news. It had spread to her liver in two spots—one on each lobe of the liver. We asked about surgery. It was not an option, the doctor said. There would be more and more treatment of chemo.

She asked to go to Halifax where two of her daughters lived. Her doctor agreed and got it all set up for her.

While in Halifax, her doctors asked her if she would go on an experimental drug. She said, "Yes, it might not help me, but someday it might help one of my children."

I visited her a couple times while she was in Halifax. We had some laughs. We had some tears, and we talked a lot about God. She was losing her hair. It was falling out. So I suggested she get it cut short. She agreed and had it done in the hospital, but even the short hair was falling out, so she told me to go get the nurse and ask her to bring in the razor. She wanted it all off. What a brave woman.

She continued to take treatment for a couple of years. She would call me and tell me, "Marilyn, it is smaller. My tumors are shrinking." She was so hopeful and happy. The drug was working.

I would call her every Sunday afternoon, put on our local church channel, and then I would put her on the speaker phone, and we would listen to a church service in La Scie every Sunday. She loved it, and I was happy I could make her happy.

I remember in 1997 when we had our Come Home Year, she came home and when everyone saw her, they were hugging her. She was so scared because she was taking treatment and was supposed to avoid people as she may catch something and that would bring her down.

That night, there was a dance on the wharf. She wasn't sure that she felt well enough to go, but she wanted to. We brought over a blanket for her to sit on, and she dressed warm. I went to the band and asked them to play her favorite song, "Row No. 2, Seat No. 3." Her friend from Burgeo asked her to dance, and she did. She was a great dancer. She and her husband could do the Newfoundland waltz. So beautiful, and with her friend, they waltzed her song. While they were waltzing, everybody on the wharf formed a circle around them. It was her night, a night I will never forget.

We took up a collection that night of $1,000 and gave it to her and her husband—just a little help. She did not want to take it, but we insisted. Grand Bruit was always known for helping the people who lived there by collecting money or through different groups making donations to help.

My sister-in-law continued to do an experimental treatment in Halifax for a couple of years. She would call me, all so excited when she had her scan, telling me the tumors on her liver were getting smaller. We prayed hard for them to be gone and give her back her life. I wanted her around for a long time, but she always said, "I'm doing this to help me, but if it won't, maybe one of these days it will help one of my children or grandchildren." She was very brave.

As the years went by, she got worse instead of better. She asked me to come to her house one day, and she showed me this beautiful dress she had worn to her niece's wedding. She told me, "I want this put on me with my red coat when I die." She said, "I have told no one else, and you make sure you do this, OK?" It broke my heart, but I agreed. We talked about death a lot. She asked me, "How do I know that I will go to heaven?" I asked her, "You do believe there is a God?" She said, "Yes." Then I asked her, "You have asked God to forgive you for everything?" She said, "Yes." And then I told her, "You have no worries about going to heaven. You have been good to other people all your life. You have faith, you know in your heart there is a God." Then I remember saying, "Save a place for me next to you." She said, "I will, right beside me."

In October 23, 2000, my sister-in-law passed away in Halifax. Her husband and I were with her. She didn't want her children to see her die. They got there about fifteen minutes later. They were so upset to lose their mom, but after a few days, they got used to it and accepted that she was not suffering no more. They then prepared for the long trip home to Grand Bruit for their mom's place of eternal rest.

As life went on in Grand Bruit, news of people being lonely seem to be more talked about. In winter, there was no one around, in summer there were lots of summer people. Lots of company for everybody. People went to their cabins on weekends, the fishermen were busy with their lobster traps, and fishing was not bad. We lost some of our older residents, and they were missed by all. Then bad news struck again a couple of years later: another sister-in-law had been told she had breast cancer. Her husband was devastated. He wished it on himself, but she said, "No."

It was a bad kind of breast cancer. She had her breast taken off quickly, and I spent some time with her in Corner Brook. It was a long time before she could talk about it or even read the books they gave her. She had to accept it before she could move on.

She took her chemo. Her radiation went through, losing her hair, but did this stop her from working? No. She was a very strong woman who worked hard all her life. Her husband was crippled with arthritis and couldn't do a lot. She would, with help, bring all freight to the store on bike, unload it, and he would pack it up. They worked well together, but he always felt guilty because she did so much. But it brought them very close to one another.

It was so interesting how my sister-in-law did all this work to help her husband, and when she got sick, it turned around completely. He took such good care of her. He helped her with her work, which was not easy working on the wharf, caring for the fish the fishermen brought in, from weighing, packing, and shipping it out. She worked very hard, and her husband worked right by her side.

After a while, he closed his store. She gave up her job, and he took care of all her needs. He did everything for her. As the months went by, her scans revealed more cancer. It upset the whole family. Her daughter was pregnant with her second child. The first child, being their only grandchild, was their pride and joy, and the little girl loved them so much.

She wanted so bad to be here when her baby grandchild was born. Her daughter would call some of us to see how we felt her mom was doing. She talked to her dad and brother every couple of hours, and eventually, as her mom got worse, she left Alberta with her little girl and came home in April.

She stayed with her mom and dad wherever they were. She travelled with them as her cousin, and many of us took care of her little girl. She took her mom to many doctor's appointments. She did what she could for her mom. Her mom spent a lot of time in bed. Her husband wanted her to be as comfortable as he could make her. He had a special memory foam brought for her to lay on. Her husband tended to her every need.

She lost a lot of weight, but no matter how she felt, she never once complained. Her granddaughter spent hours and hours playing on her bed and lying next to her nan whom she loved and adored.

Bruce was getting ready to go to Alberta to work. He didn't want to leave because he knew his sister was getting worse. He went to her house to talk to her, and she told him, "Go on, my son." He hugged her, told her he loved her. They cried together, then he left the next day.

That week, she got sicker, and her husband and daughter took her to Port aux Basques. Her son put her on the four-wheel trike and took her to the ferry. She was so brave. She looked around as she was thinking, *I might not come back alive.* And people like that, know that. They know how they feel, but she had no regrets, that's for sure. She had a good husband, good children, and she had a good family of brothers and sisters. They loved her very much.

She was not gone to Port aux Basques very long before I felt I wanted to go up and spend time with her as well. I had a chance to go to work for my friend for two weeks on night shift, which gave me time to spend all day with my sister-in-law. She had many people come to see her. Her sister came every day with her husband and sat with her. A lot of friends came by to spend time with her. She was well-loved by all.

It wasn't too long after that she got sicker every day, and she knew it. Her daughter and I were with her one day, and I asked if she was ready to go. She said, "Yes, they can't do nothing else for me." She said, "All I want is for Reanna to be OK, and I know she is." Her daughter told her mom, "I promise you, she will be OK." We had our cry, and she felt better.

A couple of days later, after going to Corner Brook for a doctor's visit, she passed away at 5:00 p.m. on June 6, 2006, or shortly after. Her little granddaughter had gone with me to get some supper at my friend's house. We just left the hospital fifteen minutes. That little girl was heartbroken for many days and months to come.

As adults, we knew and understood more, but she never could understand why Nanny was gone. Her family took her to Grand Bruit for her final journey home.

For days after, her granddaughter had to go visit her nanny, and she was very sad. She cried so hard every time she went. She had so much grief in her little body. She still, today, misses her nan, but her baby sister, who came a few weeks later, never got to know Nanny, but I am sure she knows all about her through her sister, her mom, and her poppy.

If she were alive today, she would be, once again, a happy woman, knowing she has a little grandson and her son was so happy with his partner and baby boy. She worried about her son, wondering if he would settle down. Well, he did, with a good job and a beautiful family. She would be so content.

Grand Bruit began to get very lonely, as I said before. Our kids were growing up and leaving home. School was becoming less and less—from two teachers down to one; from twenty kids, down to six. Teachers came and went. Some loved Grand Bruit, some were a bit bored. It was an outport community, not much going for young teachers. If they wanted to go to a movie or just to go out, they went away on weekends when the weather was good. Just for a change.

We had one teacher come from Corner Brook. The kids loved her, and all people of Grand Bruit liked her as well. She did different things with the kids and most of the time included the community in things she had planned. We were there for one year while she was teaching there, so I got to know her. I knew her parents before as her dad taught school in Burgeo.

She went through a rough time. While there, her sister got sick, and she had to leave for a while, so they sent someone in her place for a short while. The kids couldn't wait for her to come back.

She was there for two years. She then went to teach in Burnt Islands, and on her way home on a weekend, she was tragically killed in a car accident. Grand Bruit was devastated over losing a beautiful young woman in her thirties. She will never be forgotten. She was the last teacher who taught in Grand Bruit. I wrote her a letter and told her I was so happy that she was our last teacher, and God knew what he was doing putting her there. Our children ended their school days very happily because of the teacher they had. It was sad that our school was closing.

Things started to go downhill after our school closed, or at least that's my opinion. No more kids in Grand Bruit, only on weekends or Christmas and Easter for holidays.

Not enough people to play darts or card games no more. The word of resettlement started to float around when people were talking. They all knew there was more to life outside of Grand Bruit, but it would die down for a while because some people, at first, did not want to hear about it.

Yes, in summer we had lots and lots of company, people coming and going every day. Summer homes were full all summer long, relatives came to visit, and the bed and breakfast was overbooked most of the time. Kids were everywhere. The sounds in Grand Bruit were so nice. You could sit on your bridge, close your eyes, and listen to the children walking and chatting as they go, making plans for that night.

You could hear men talking about their day of fishing. I open my eyes, and I see some lady in her summer home, hanging her clothes on the line. I close my eyes again, and I hear the buzz of the whipper snipper—our lady who loves to cut grass as she cuts the grass all over.

I loved sitting or lying on my bridge, listening to these sounds. I could hear someone starting their boat. Grand Bruit was alive in the summer.

Our lady from the USA, with her husband, would drive up the road in her scooter with him walking alongside. My neighbor as well had a scooter because he found it more and more difficult to walk as he got older. He and his wife would sit for hours on their bridge, day after day, night after night. They both would turn brown on their faces and arms from being outdoors so much. They had no children, but loved it when people stopped to have a chat and lean across the rail for a while, just to keep up on the latest gossip.

She became very ill with breast cancer once again. A few women in Grand Bruit came down with this dreaded sickness. She went through the whole treatment process, and she was good for a while, but after a while, the cancer took her, and she passed away.

Another one gone from Grand Bruit, her husband then became very lonely. He was well taken care of by his sister-in-law who fed him and made sure he was. His brother did what he needed to be done. His sister, in the summer, took care of him when she was home.

Our population was going down more and more. People were scared to talk about moving. Scared it would upset people, but we could do nothing about what was happening to Grand Bruit.

A lot of people thought the older residents would be the ones to be most upset about resettling. Then again, we never had anybody pass seventy years of age no more.

Grand Bruit was not the same with people leaving because of the closing of the mine Hope Brook, and my husband and I were two people who did not have a choice. We could have made the choice to stay home and seek other means of income, like social services, but that was not in us as we were both in good health.

With many people dying, young and old alike, it took our community down at lot. In 1997, we left Grand Bruit with a heavy heart. As the years came and went and the more people I talked to from home, the lonelier they sounded. I would talk to my sister-in-law, and she would tell me, "I don't see no one, except my son and his family." She would say, "I look through my window for an hour at a time, and there is no one to be seen, not a soul." She said, "I can't spend another lonely winter here in Grand Bruit no more. It breaks my heart, but I will go crazy if I have to stay another winter here." And it was understandable that she was lonely after her husband passed away.

We would go home to visit whenever we could. We made sure that while we were home, we went and spent time with all our relatives. Bruce went home to hunt, fish, and as we spent time with our relatives, they would each bring up how lonely they were. There was sadness in their eyes. They felt their life was slipping away. They had too much time to think, and they missed their spouses so much.

They would tell me that when they went for a walk, they met no one.

There were some people who were against leaving. They were happy with the life they had. Their words were "what do we want with any more than what we got?" They had a right to feel the way they did as people had the right to feel they wanted more.

It brought a lot of bad feelings among the people at first. Some didn't think they could have a life outside of Grand Bruit. They would miss the beauty and peace and quiet, but what they didn't realize was that whatever they had in Grand Bruit, they could have elsewhere.

After a while, the idea got around that most people wanted to move, so the government was contacted through our MHA, Mr. Kelvin Parsons. He was advising all of us on what route this would take and it would not happen overnight. He said he would arrange a meeting in Grand Bruit for all people to attend and ask the questions that we had.

In the meantime, the local district committee decided to go out with a bang and planned, once again, a Come Home Year—our last ever to be in Grand Bruit.

As the word went out about the resettlement, the word went out about the Come Home Year. People from our past, people who knew Grand Bruit existed, wanted to come because it would be their last visit. Word spread like wildfire about the resettlement. People in Grand Bruit got phone calls from people they had not heard from in years.

The bed and breakfast was overbooked with tourists who had heard about the resettlement, reading about it in the local papers, reading about it online. They were sad for the community, but happy for the people who wanted it.

A lot of our relatives didn't understand why people wanted to leave, and some made it known to the people of Grand Bruit. Our own son didn't like the idea at all. He was so upset. Bruce himself felt the same way.

But like one wise person of Grand Bruit said, "It is OK for people to get upset, they don't live here all year around. They come for a visit and then they leave. They have another life somewhere else." That was a true statement. The people of Grand Bruit were always there. A very different life than the people who came and left.

Finally, a meeting was held at Grand Bruit. Everybody in the community attended. They told us what it meant to be resettled, what it took, and what we had to do, and what amount of money was offered to each family.

Then it was open for questions. I asked, "What about us? We had to leave because of work." He told me we were in the gray area, but each family would speak on behalf of themselves with the government. We all would have the chance to plead our cases. We were happy with their answers.

So the process of the resettlement took place with the community getting a lawyer on our behalf, and the government offered to pay for the lawyer, which I thought was very good of them.

Many papers came and were filled out by all people—summer and permanent residents. Everybody who knew people from Grand Bruit had their opinion on everybody else. The people of Grand Bruit had strong opinions on who should and would qualify for what amount of money they thought people should get.

A lot of people outside of Grand Bruit expressed their words. Some were very upset, hearing all kinds of rumors. Believe you me, a lot of rumors went around.

It was not up to the people of Grand Bruit or outside of Grand Bruit to decide who got what.

The government had criteria to be met, and if a family met those criteria, then you were considered a permanent resident. The government did their work, and they did it good. They had the final say.

When we went home for a visit, that was all that was talked about, and it was told to me plain and blunt, "You don't deserve the full amount."

I would not get angry or upset. I just said that decision is in the hands of the government, and I am happy I never got mad. I didn't want bad friends. Once you burn bridges, you can't rebuild them.

I treated everyone the same. I said, "It will all work out, and whatever the government gives us, we will be happy with."

After one, two, and three years, the time came for the final meeting. It was held at the school, and everybody attended. You could feel the stress of all. The government members, plus our lawyer attended and asked us to please give him time to speak, and he would take questions after.

I have to commend the government. They had their work done. They had taken everything into the fact of who qualified and who didn't.

Everyone was stressed. No one wanted a fuss, and there wasn't. When questions started, it got a bit heated by some who didn't get their own way, but once again, our government members and lawyer handled it so well.

Some voices were raised in defense of the questions that were asked, but the people who asked the questions had a right to, as one woman stated when a man could not understand her reason for wanting to move. She told him, "You only come to Grand Bruit for a month in summer, we live here all year around. Why don't you move here, all summer people, then we wouldn't need to move."

An excellent statement indeed. My dear, only people who lived in Grand Bruit all year around knew how lonely it was. They wanted more and wanted to enjoy life.

Now the work started for the local service district committee. Grand Bruit had to be packed up from their own houses to the committee, doing the church and everything the local service owned. Packing, selling items, doing the books, shipping all items out, making decisions of what communities got what—it was a lot of work, and it was done by a few people. They were so tired, but they did an awesome job, and all communities east and west of Grand Bruit got a little piece of Grand Bruit.

Communities from La Poile to Grey River got a piece of Grand Bruit from things that came from our fire hall to things that came from our church. Grand Bruit will live on in those communities.

There were only a few who took on the job of packing up Grand Bruit. We had an awesome lawyer from Port aux Basques who was gentle, compassionate, and treated us with respect at all times. The men from municipal affairs were the same. If we had questions we needed answers to, they answered them. They did their work, and they handled it great.

It was so sad to see our ferry leaving Grand Bruit packed full of people's belongings. Some of the men carried things in their boats. Everyone was busy. They were all excited about the life that was coming but very sad about leaving Grand Bruit.

The last church service took place. Ministers came in to close our church down. I could not make it to the service due to work commitments, but Bruce went, and he phoned me as soon as it was over. He said it was so sad, and the church was packed full.

Time came and went, people left and settled into their new homes in Burgeo and Port aux Basques.

Everyone received their money, what the government thought they deserved. There were a lot of unhappy people among them who spent summers in Grand Bruit and thought they should have gotten more.

The government had a set of questions for everyone. If you qualified for the full amount, you got it. If not, you got what you qualified for. The government did their work and took into consideration a lot of things. If people left Grand Bruit, what was the reason why? If someone was sick, if students had to leave.

Even though a lot of people had different opinions on what everyone should get, they could not change nothing. The government had the final say.

The ferry left Grand Bruit for the last time on June 30, 2010.

And today, as I think back over the years I spent in Grand Bruit, I remember my life, and I never regretted one day living there and bringing our family up the best way we could. They never had the best of everything, but they had love and discipline and plenty to eat. It was a privilege to live in Grand Bruit for twenty-one years. I will sum up a few things I remember and loved:

1) My mother-in-law living with us for a couple of winters until she remembered very little.
2) My father-in-law, who loved playing crib—his game of cards.
3) My neighbor, who loved visitors, and her husband singing hymns and the sound of his voice coming through my windows.
4) The kids my children had as cousins and friends, and this remains the same today, connected by Grand Bruit.
5) The two grocery stores that did their best to get what you needed or wanted, even if they didn't sell it.
6) Our school and the teachers who touched my life over the years, and once again, are still in my life.
7) Our church was special to me. We did not get to go to church very often, but the church is God's house, and God is everywhere.

8) The older ladies who were my neighbors. I would visit often, and one of them was a very talented sewing woman. Together, they would have a few differences of opinion, but they always remained friends until the day they died.
9) Bruce's aunt and uncle who had the beautiful flower garden every summer and who loved to walk to the hills every day.
10) How the men all got together in winter and shovelled the snow off the roads so the kids on the side would not fall and go over the falls.
11) My best friend and sister-in-law who hung around with me but could never keep a secret, who played cards with us on Saturday nights, and whom we had good laughs with.
12) My brother-in-law who loved watching TV in silence and serving drinks to our husbands.
13) My sister-in-law who, every Sunday night, prepared a dinner for us and gave us our own mugs, which she would not let anyone else use.
14) Our other sister-in-law who we visited every Sunday night, and who had coffee ready for us, which most nights we never had even though she had it ready.

15) My aunts and uncle who I loved to visit.
16) I remember all the good times—the weddings, the New Year's balls, the summer people coming home. Life was good in Grand Bruit for a long time.

But looking back in 1997 or a couple years before, when the government encouraged us to travel more because we had better boat service, I truly believe they had in their minds then that after a while, people will move, and a community that cost so much for medical and ferry service plus a few other facts will be no more. I think, back in 1997, that was the hidden agenda.

Well, nowadays, there are no children, no adults. Our relatives who are in Grand Bruit to stay are in the cemetery. There are no lights, no sounds, and no life left there. It is very sad to say, but Grand Bruit is now silent.

CPSIA information can be obtained at www.ICGtesting.com
Printed in the USA
LVOW101937300413

331652LV00001B/331/P